To Bob Lister, Grant Bage, Will Griffiths
and all at the Cambridge Schools Classics Project— H. L. and D. M.

To MeliNeo, FifiRuben & LiliTom — C. H.

THE ADVENTURES OF
ACHILLES

Barefoot Books
2067 Massachusetts Ave
Cambridge, MA 02140

Text copyright © 2012 by Hugh Lupton and
Daniel Morden
Illustrations copyright © 2012 by Carole Hénaff
The moral rights of Hugh Lupton, Daniel Morden
and Carole Hénaff have been asserted
Narrated by Hugh Lupton and Daniel Morden
Recorded and mixed by Dylan Fowler at
Stiwdio Felin Fach, Abergavenny, Wales

First published in the United States by
Barefoot Books, Inc in 2012

Graphic design by Judy Linard, London
Color separation by B & P International, Hong Kong
Printed in China on 100% acid-free paper
This book was typeset in Caslon Old Face 14 on 20
point, Galahad, Lithos Regular and Trajan
The illustrations were prepared in acrylics

ISBN 978-1-84686-420-9

Library of Congress Cataloging-in-Publication
Data is available under LCCN 2011044731

1 3 5 7 9 8 6 4 2

Bibliography

Calasso, Roberto. *The Marriage of Cadmus and Harmony*. New York: Vintage, 1994.

Graves, Robert. *The Greek Myths*. New York: Penguin, 1960.

Homer. *The Iliad*. Robert Fagles, translator. New York: Viking, 1990.

Lancelyn Green, Roger. *The Tale of Troy*. London: Puffin, 1958.

March, Jenny. *Cassell's Dictionary of Classical Mythology*. London: Cassell Reference, 1998.

Schwab, Gustav. *Gods and Heroes*. New York: Pantheon, 1974.

*Although Greek and Trojan warriors in the Bronze Age generally wore armor made of
bronze and other metals, the illustrator of this book made a stylistic choice to
depict the warriors in colorful armor to draw the contrast between
the Greek and Trojan armies.*

THE ADVENTURES OF ACHILLES

Retold by HUGH LUPTON and DANIEL MORDEN

Illustrated by CAROLE HÉNAFF

Barefoot Books
step inside a story

·CONTENTS·

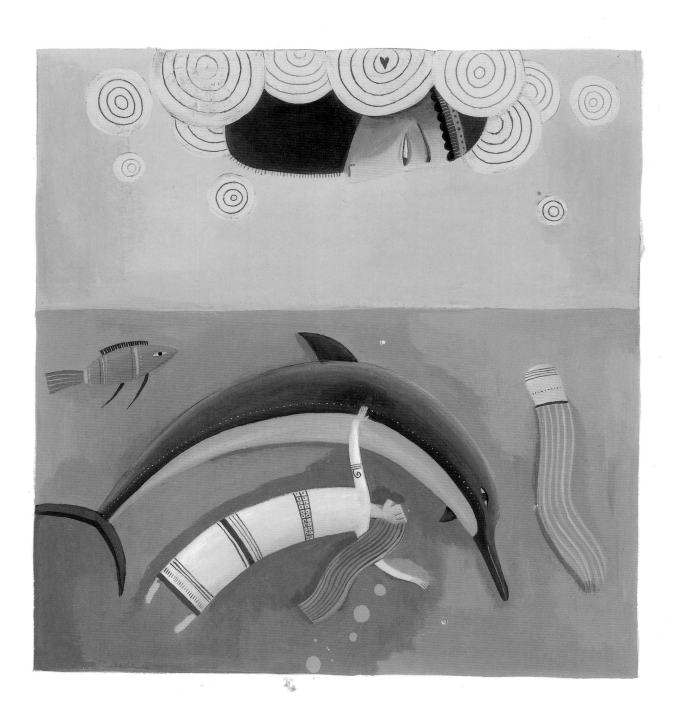

·THE·SEEDS·OF·LOVE·

·7·

There was once an impossible mountain, a mountain so vast that no mortal ever saw its summit. It was called Mount Olympus. It was the home of the undying gods, the immortals.

Zeus, king of all immortals, sat in his throne on Mount Olympus. The earth was spread out before him. Nothing was hidden from his view. He was fascinated by the stories that unfolded beneath him. Zeus whiled away whole centuries watching the little figures scurrying to their deaths.

He took to watching a nymph who liked to visit a beach on an island in the blue Aegean Sea. Every morning she would ride a dolphin to the shallows, wade up the incline, lie on her belly in the white sand and fall asleep. Zeus became consumed with desire for her. He summoned his brother, the sea god Poseidon.

"Who is she?" asked Zeus.

"Her name is Thetis," said Poseidon. "Surely you know of her. It is said that one day she'll have a son who will grow up to be greater than his father."

Zeus had overthrown his own father, Cronos. He had no desire to suffer the same fate at the hands of one of his sons. How could he lie with her without putting himself in danger?

A shining thought entered Zeus's mind. He'd find a mortal husband for Thetis. She'd have a son by him. The child would grow up to be greater than his human father, and Zeus would be free to lie with her to his heart's content.

The mighty gods can disguise themselves as mortals. Zeus transformed himself so that to all the world he was a nobleman. He traveled to the court of a Greek king whose name was Peleus. He was one of the Argonauts who'd sailed with Jason. Peleus was a fierce man, skilled in the arts of battle. He wore his livid scars as a queen wears her jewels.

Zeus carried himself well. Peleus was impressed by his bearing and welcomed him with a lavish feast. After the feast, Zeus made a gesture in the air. An image appeared before Peleus: the image of an island in the blue Aegean Sea. Peleus saw a female figure approaching the island, riding a dolphin as though it was a pony. She waded up the shallows, lay on her belly in the white sand and fell asleep.

Peleus was filled with love and desire. He cursed under his breath. He had been overtaken by this vision. His actions were no longer in his control. He couldn't help himself. He was infatuated with this nymph. It was as though he was under a spell.

"Who is she?" asked Peleus.

"Her name is Thetis," said Zeus. "I'll tell you where you'll find her."

Peleus found to his dismay that he had no choice but to seek out Thetis. Immediately he began preparations. He set out on his voyage as soon as the tide would allow. He sailed to the island he'd seen in his vision. He laid out lavish gifts on the beach.

A shape appeared between sea and sky.

The sea nymph Thetis saw a man gesturing to her from the island. Warily, she climbed from her dolphin and waded through the shallows. She saw trinkets laid out in the sand. The great warrior king Peleus blushed, stumbled and mumbled words of love.

"You can have me if you can catch me," said Thetis.

He laughed. Then lunged.

Peleus's arms were around a seagull that pecked at his eyes with its sharp beak and gouged a chunk out of his cheek. Then Thetis was a swallow, darting out of his grasp. By pure luck he managed to grab her – and found himself wrapped around an enormous eel. He knew if she reached the ocean she would be free. He gripped her tightly and found himself clutching a lioness that struck him with her paw, scratched him with her claw. He fell. She leapt into the sea as a seal. They stared at one another, Peleus, panting, staunching the wound in his cheek. Thetis held his gaze so long with her wet-pebble eyes that Peleus took some comfort. Then she turned to the open sea, and she was gone.

That night, Peleus lit a fire on the island and made offerings. Then he shouted to the stars.

"You, stranger, you who came to my palace. If you are who I think you are, help me now!"

There was a blast of light before him. Peleus turned his face away. His ears were singing. Even with his eyes closed he could see the figure emerging from the light. It was Hermes, the messenger of the gods. Peleus knew him by his winged sandals.

Hermes grinned. "This is what you must do."

The next morning Thetis returned. She saw no footprints in the sand. She climbed from the back of her dolphin and waded up the shallows. She searched her beach. Nothing. No one. She lay on her belly in the white sand and fell asleep.

Peleus had been hiding in the branches of a tree. He climbed down the tree and crept across the beach. Carefully, tenderly, he tied her hands and feet behind her back with a rope.

Thetis awoke with a jerk. The rope bit into her skin. Instantly she knew Peleus had outwitted her. If she were to transform herself into an animal, she would tear her body in two. Her shoulders slumped.

Peleus approached. He knelt. He untied her wrists and ankles. He rubbed them. Thetis rolled onto her back, drew his head to hers and kissed him.

·A·WEDDING·AND·A·BIRTH·
·13·

On the night of the next full moon, Peleus and Thetis were married in a clearing on that island. The nine Muses sang. All the immortals brought wonderful gifts.

The first to present her gift was the goddess of war and wisdom, owl-eyed Athene. She gave them a spear so sharp it could draw blood from the wind.

Then Ares, god of battle, gave them a golden breastplate emblazoned with silver stars.

The goddess of love, Aphrodite, took from her finger a golden ring cast in the shape of a curling arrow, whose sharp point touched its feathered tail.

The god of the sea, Poseidon, gave four white horses that once had been the crests of waves, four white horses whose father had been the West Wind.

Zeus transformed a nest of ants into an army. Their bodies were the bodies of men, but their minds were the minds of ants. They were black-eyed, black-toothed, black-tongued, black-armored. They were silent, implacable, obedient. They would never lose heart, doubt, tire or feel fear. They were called the Myrmidons and they were the most terrifying army in the world.

The last god to give a gift was Hades, the god of the dead. Hades gave the couple a black urn.

Inlaid in silver across its front was an image of three ancient sisters: the three Fates.

The first sister, who spins out the thread of a mortal life.

The second, who measures out the length of the life.

The third, who cuts the thread and ends the life.

King Peleus and Thetis gave thanks for their wonderful gifts. They clasped hands. They danced. And all around them, in a looping, curling spiral, mortal and immortal danced together in harmony.

Far above, on Mount Olympus, one solitary goddess sneered. Eris had not received an invitation to the wedding. She never did. She was the goddess of strife. Where she went, discord and argument followed. The gorge rose in the back of her throat. All this joy and harmony was nauseating to her.

"Everyone else has given a gift," said Eris. "Why should I not do the same?" She dropped something. It fell through the clouds. It landed in the center of the clearing, at the feet of the bride and groom.

The music stopped. All eyes were on Peleus. He knelt. He lifted the object from the grass . . .

"A golden apple!" he said. "A golden apple has fallen from the heavens!" He turned it in his palm. "There are words on the skin. 'To the fairest.' I must give this apple to the most beautiful of all of you."

Three goddesses stood before Peleus. Each one had stretched out her hand. Each thought herself the most beautiful. Each expected to be given the apple that instant.

There was owl-eyed Athene, goddess of war and wisdom. Standing beside her was the wife of Zeus, ox-eyed Hera. And beside her stood Aphrodite, the goddess of love.

King Peleus swallowed. He was in mortal danger. To choose one goddess was to insult the other two. Those whom he had slighted would turn against him. They would not rest until he was dead.

Zeus stepped forward and held out his hand. Peleus dropped the apple into Zeus's palm. He slipped it into his pocket and nodded at the Muses. They sang as best they could, but it was no use. The wedding was over. All goodwill had been forgotten the moment Peleus read the words from the skin of the apple. Hera, Athene and Aphrodite whined, snapped and bickered with such vehemence that the flowers at their feet curled up and died. The grass went brown. The trees shed their leaves. A passing bird, caught in the cross fire, tumbled from the sky like a stone. Zeus soon found he had a headache.

Nine months later the sea nymph Thetis gave birth to a baby boy. She consulted an oracle. She discovered to her dismay that if the child grew up and went to war, though he would win great glory, he would die young. King Peleus was a warrior king. He would want his son to win great glory, even if that meant the boy's death.

Thetis took the baby to the end of the world. She dipped him headfirst in the dark waters of the River Styx. Wherever the water touched him, his skin became invulnerable. But there was one place the water could not reach . . . the place where she held him: his heel.

She carried the child back to her husband. Peleus was so furious that she had stolen their child away without his knowledge or permission that he banished her. From that moment the baby never had the chance to suck on his mother's breasts, so the name he was given means No Lips.

Peleus took his son to Mount Pelion to be trained by centaurs in the arts of war. He was fed on the marrow of bears to make him strong, the guts of lions to make him fierce, and the milk of deer to make him swift.

On his sixth birthday the boy killed his first wild boar. From that day, he was always dragging dying beasts into the centaurs' cave. On his twelfth birthday he chased and killed a full-grown stag.

Far away his mother heard of this. She was terrified that soon he would be sent off to some war where he would be killed. She kidnapped him again. She took him far away to the island of Skyros and dressed him as a woman. She hid him among the daughters of the king of the island. Before she left him, she slipped onto his finger the wedding gift of Aphrodite: the ring cast in the shape of a curling arrow whose sharp point touched its feathered tail.

For five years Peleus's son lived the life of a woman. During those years he became friends with a warrior named Patroclus. He gave Patroclus that golden ring. Patroclus wore it proudly: the ring given to him by his friend Achilles.

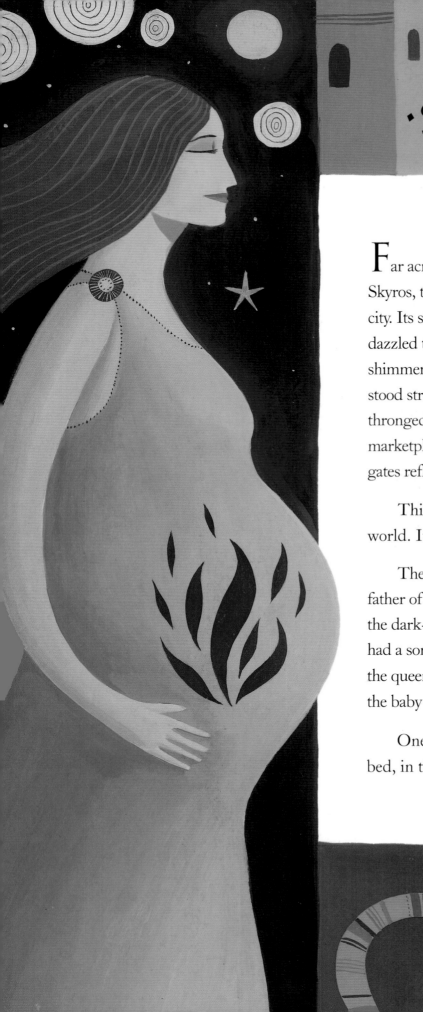

·STOLEN·LOVE·
·18·

Far across the blue Aegean Sea, far to the east of the island of Skyros, to the east of the nation of Greece, there was a magnificent city. Its stone walls stretched high into the sky. Its painted palaces dazzled the eyes of all who gazed upon them. Its marble temples shimmered with light. Its houses of timber and brick and stone stood strong and steadfast. Its broad, accommodating streets thronged with men, women, children, horses and dogs, and its marketplaces teemed with sheep, pigs and cattle. The city's bronze gates reflected the golden glow of the sun.

This was the city of Troy, the most beautiful city in the world. It had been founded by Apollo, the god of light.

The king of Troy was called Priam. He was the white-bearded father of the city. The queen of Troy was called Hecuba. She was the dark-haired mother of the city. King Priam and Queen Hecuba had a son, a strong, strapping boy whose name was Hector. And the queen was expecting a second child. Her belly was swollen with the baby she was carrying in her womb.

One night Queen Hecuba was lying fast asleep in the royal bed, in the royal bedchamber, in her painted palace, when she

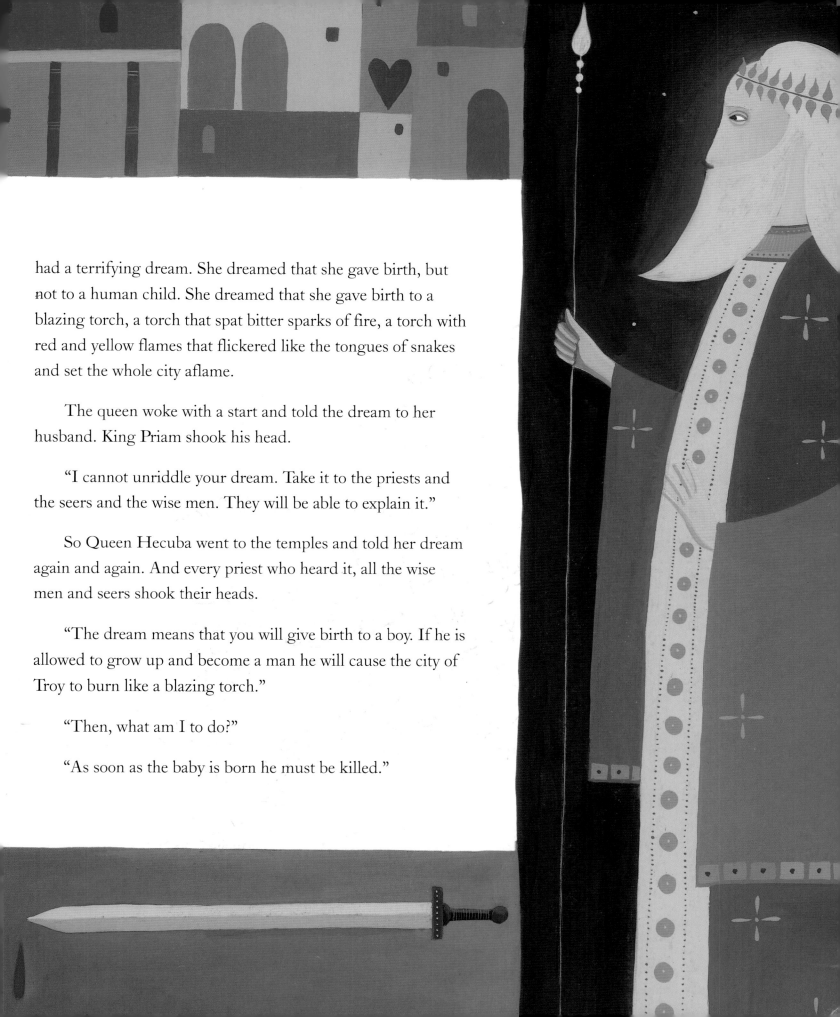

had a terrifying dream. She dreamed that she gave birth, but not to a human child. She dreamed that she gave birth to a blazing torch, a torch that spat bitter sparks of fire, a torch with red and yellow flames that flickered like the tongues of snakes and set the whole city aflame.

The queen woke with a start and told the dream to her husband. King Priam shook his head.

"I cannot unriddle your dream. Take it to the priests and the seers and the wise men. They will be able to explain it."

So Queen Hecuba went to the temples and told her dream again and again. And every priest who heard it, all the wise men and seers shook their heads.

"The dream means that you will give birth to a boy. If he is allowed to grow up and become a man he will cause the city of Troy to burn like a blazing torch."

"Then, what am I to do?"

"As soon as the baby is born he must be killed."

A few days later Queen Hecuba went into labor. The midwives were fetched and the baby was born. As had been foretold, it was a baby boy. But he was the most beautiful child. He lay in his mother's arms opening and closing his little hands. His face glowed with life and light. His perfect lips mouthed at the air as though he were hungry for life.

King Priam came striding into the bedchamber. He drew his bronze sword and lifted it above his shoulder. But he couldn't bring himself to kill the child. So he summoned his soldiers. One after another they entered the room, but even the most hardened cutthroat in his army couldn't take the life of this beautiful boy. So Priam ordered one of his cowherds to take the baby and leave him on the slopes of Mount Ida, the great snowcapped mountain that stretched high behind the city walls.

"He will be eaten by wolves or foxes, or torn apart by eagles," he said.

But the next morning, when the cowherd went back to the rock on the mountainside where he'd left the naked baby, he found the footprints of a bear. He followed the tracks to a cave. He peered inside. He saw a huge brown she-bear tenderly suckling the baby.

"Surely this baby is destined to live," he thought.

When the bear was gone he lifted the beautiful child, laid him in his leather bag (called a *paris*), and carried him back to the king. When Priam and Hecuba heard the story and saw their child, they wept with joy.

"The mighty gods and goddesses have protected him. He must be allowed to live."

Queen Hecuba looked at the leather bag he was lying in.

"And we will call him Paris."

And so Prince Paris grew up in the painted palace of King Priam and Queen Hecuba. He grew from babyhood to boyhood. He became a beautiful youth. He became a handsome young man. The priests and seers and wise men watched him growing and they shook their heads.

Seventeen years passed. And then, one day, Prince Paris was out hunting on the foothills of Mount Ida with his bow and his quiverful of arrows. As he was climbing the steep, sloping track of the mountain it so happened that great Zeus, the Cloud Compeller, glanced down from the high slopes of Mount Olympus and caught sight of him. The father of the immortals rubbed his eyes and looked again. This prince, this king's son, was as beautiful as a god. Zeus's head was still aching. Hera, Athene and Aphrodite had never stopped their bickering argument as to who deserved the golden apple. Then a shining thought entered Zeus's mind.

"This Paris, this beautiful prince, will decide once and for all."

Zeus summoned Hermes and passed him the apple. Swift as thought, the messenger of the gods swooped down from the heavens. In an instant he was standing in front of Paris.

"Paris!' said Hermes. "I have been sent by great father Zeus."

Paris recognized Hermes by his winged sandals. He dropped to his knees.

"Zeus has told me to tell you that you must decide which of these three goddesses is the most beautiful."

Hermes clicked his fingers and Paris was blinded by light. He covered his face with his hands. Slowly Paris opened his fingers and saw before him the three most powerful goddesses of all. Hermes gestured to them with his hand.

"When you have made your decision you must give the chosen one this golden apple."

Paris felt the cold weight of a golden apple against the palm of his hand. He looked down at it. When he looked up again Hermes was gone. The three goddesses glowered at him. Paris's mouth went dry. He looked from one to another, but his eyes kept wandering toward Aphrodite. Hera stamped her foot.

"It's not fair," she said. "Aphrodite is wearing her girdle of love and desire. Paris must decide when he's seen us naked."

Athene agreed. And so the three goddesses shed their shimmering robes, until they were standing stark naked. Paris stared wide-eyed from one goddess to another, but now he could not decide who was the most beautiful.

Ox-eyed Hera, the magnificent queen of Heaven, stepped forward.

"Paris," she whispered, "choose me and I will give you power. Choose me and I will make you a great king over Europe and Asia. Half the world will be yours."

She stepped back. Athene came forward, her gray eyes blazing with light, her long limbs unblemished.

"Paris, choose me and you will never lose a battle. Choose me and you will be famous the length and the breadth of the world for your wisdom."

She stepped back. Aphrodite came forward, smelling of musk and honey. Her voice was deep and enchanting.

"Paris, choose me and I will give you the most beautiful woman in the world."

"Who is she?" whispered Paris.

"Her name is Helen," said Aphrodite. "She is the wife of red-haired Menelaus, the king of Sparta. I will blind her with love for you. She will give you everything."

"What does she look like?"

Aphrodite smiled. "She is as beautiful as I."

Such words in the ears of a seventeen-year-old prince were more than he could resist. The choice was clear as daylight. Paris lifted the golden apple above his shoulder and lowered it onto a waiting palm.

"The golden apple goes to Aphrodite," he said.

Hera and Athene turned on their heels and disappeared in a flash into the sky. They were furious. Already they were pondering in their hearts how they could bring about the death of Paris and the destruction of the city of Troy.

Prince Paris, dazed and confused, returned to Troy. And a few days later, as chance would have it (if there is such a thing as chance when three goddesses have set their inscrutable gaze on any mortal), Paris was asked by his father, King Priam, to travel to Sparta and deliver a message to red-haired Menelaus.

Before the sun had set, the prow of Paris's ship was cutting a path across the blue waves of the Aegean Sea. He journeyed for a week until he reached the shores of Sparta. He traveled overland to the palace of Menelaus. Soon the red-haired king was welcoming him to his feasting hall. Meat and bread, wine and honey cakes were set before him. Paris began to eat.

But he'd barely taken three mouthfuls when the door opened and Menelaus's wife entered the room. She sat opposite Paris at the table. Their eyes met. And at that moment the goddess of love told her son, sure-sighted Eros, to loose two invisible arrows.

Paris fell in love with Helen. And Helen fell in love with Paris. They couldn't help themselves. It was beyond their control.

The next day the two stole what treasures they could from Menelaus's palace and hurried overland to their waiting ship. They lifted anchor and sailed away. But they didn't go far. They stopped at the island of Cranae and lay down together on the soft grass, each one lost in the other's beauty. From Cranae they made a slow journey homeward, stopping again and again, until it was said that there wasn't one single island between Sparta and Troy where Paris and Helen had not lain in one another's arms.

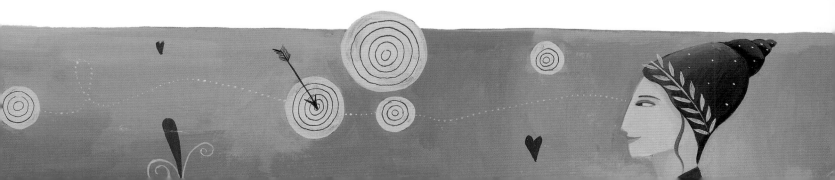

·THE·SEEDS·OF·WAR·
·27·

When Menelaus discovered that the coffers of his treasure room were empty, when he found his wife stolen by that pretty Trojan prince, he was furious. Trembling with anger he traveled to the palace of his brother, Agamemnon, the high king of all Greece.

"Years ago," said Menelaus, "when we Greek kings first heard of Helen's beauty, we traveled to the palace of her foster father, hoping to win her hand in marriage. He led a stallion into the feasting hall and slaughtered it before us. He cut it into pieces, and laid the pieces across the floor. Each of us had to stand on a piece of that stallion and promise that when Helen chose a husband we would abide by her decision, and if ever she was taken from him we would come to his aid. That day Helen walked through the blood and took my hand. She chose me. The time has come to make the other kings keep the promise they made. We will muster an army the likes of which the world has never seen, and we will bring back my wife, even if we have to level the city to do so!"

Agamemnon was less anxious to risk life and limb. After all, it wasn't his wife who had been stolen. He sent envoys to Troy demanding that Helen be returned. Unfortunately they reached the city long before Paris and Helen, who were making a leisurely progress across the sea, stopping at every island. The envoys returned to Greece with this message:

"I, Priam, father of Troy, know nothing of this Helen. But if my son has chosen to take her from you, it must have been with good reason and I will defend his decision no matter what the cost."

Agamemnon had no choice then but to send messengers to the many Greek kings, ordering them to prepare for war. All over that great nation, armies were mustered and high-prowed ships were built.

Agamemnon had a prophet. His name was Calchas. He announced that the Greeks would only be successful in their venture if they had among their number the son of warlike Peleus and the sea nymph Thetis.

"The boy Achilles must be part of your army," said Calchas.

Achilles's father was keen for him to go to fight, but his mother, fearful of some prophecy, had kidnapped him. Rumor had it he was hidden on the island of Skyros.

Agamemnon ordered a cunning king called Odysseus to find and fetch Achilles. Though this king was only nineteen years old, and ruled only a little rocky outpost of an island to the west, he was already famous for his nimble wits. Odysseus disguised himself, his crew and his ship as though they were a company of merchants. Then he traveled across the sea to Skyros. He searched the court of the king of Skyros with no success. The next morning he went to the harbor and spoke to his crew.

"I go now to the palace of the princess. Give me the morning, then I need you to make the sounds of an invasion. Smash your swords against your shields. Blow your trumpets."

Then Odysseus, as a merchant, went to the palace of the princess. He asked for an empty room. He covered the floor with merchant's goods – bolts of embroidered cloth, fine rugs, clothes, food, wine, ornaments, jewelry . . . Under one of the rugs he slid a battered, blunt sword. He told the servants to fetch the princess and her friends.

The women fell upon the wonderful wares. They tasted the food and wine, they passed the jewelry from hand to hand . . . they were surprised to see among these precious things a battered, blunt sword. They paid it no heed.

Then, from the harbor below, there came the sound of swords clashed against shields, the blowing of bronze trumpets. The island was under attack! All the women turned to the princess, unsure as to what to do . . . except one. One beautiful woman knelt, peeled back the corner of the rug, grabbed the battered sword and rushed outside to attack the invaders.

Odysseus followed her. He put his hand on her shoulder. She turned, the sword above her head, her eyes blazing.

"You're Achilles!" said Odysseus, "I've found you. Listen to me. War is coming. A great crime has been committed against us Greeks. To right this wrong we need you. Agamemnon, the high king of all Greece, sent me to find you! If you join our cause, you will be the greatest warrior in the greatest army in the history of the world. Men and women will tell stories of your adventures for as long as there are people on the earth!"

Such words in the ears of the seventeen-year-old prince were too powerful to resist. Achilles took off the clothes of women. He dressed himself instead as a warrior. He and

Patroclus sailed across the sea to the palace of Achilles's father. Warlike Peleus gave his son all the fateful wedding gifts:

The spear that could draw blood from the wind.

The golden breastplate emblazoned with silver stars.

The four white horses that once had been the crests of waves.

The ant army, the Myrmidons.

And the black urn. The gift of the last of all gods, Hades. Inlaid across its front there was an image of the three Fates.

The first sister, who spins out the thread of a life.

The second, who measures out its length.

And the third, who cuts the thread and ends the life.

Achilles and Patroclus prepared to go to war.

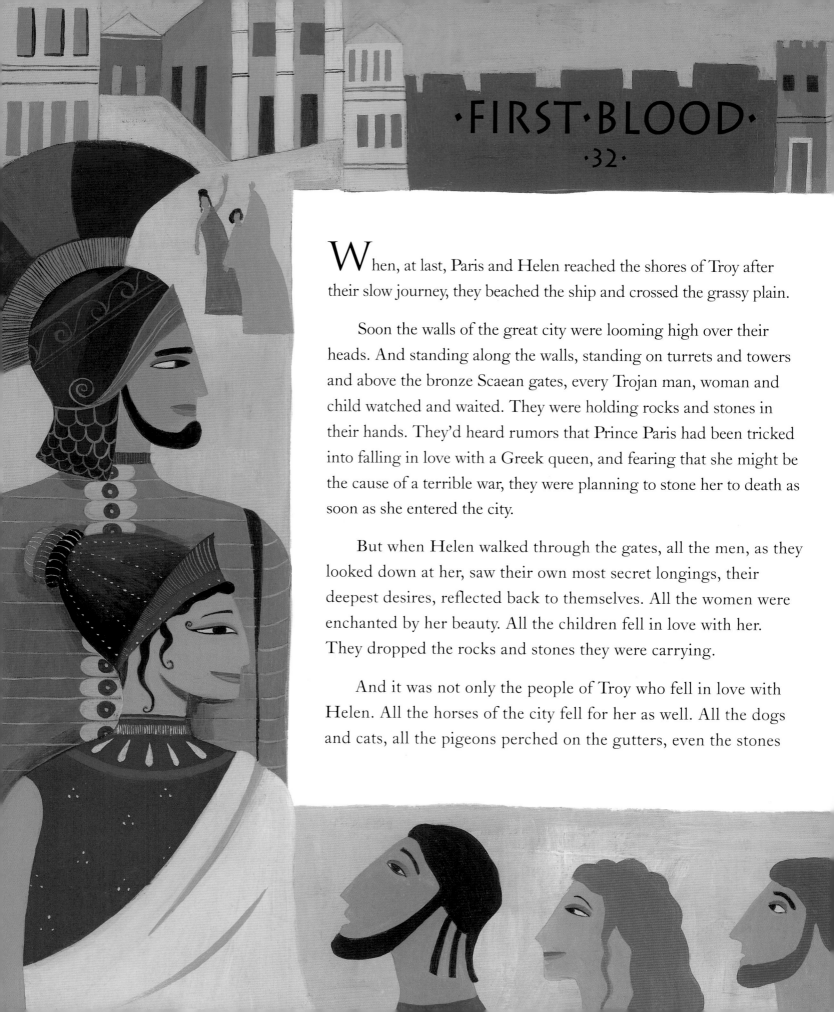

When, at last, Paris and Helen reached the shores of Troy after their slow journey, they beached the ship and crossed the grassy plain.

Soon the walls of the great city were looming high over their heads. And standing along the walls, standing on turrets and towers and above the bronze Scaean gates, every Trojan man, woman and child watched and waited. They were holding rocks and stones in their hands. They'd heard rumors that Prince Paris had been tricked into falling in love with a Greek queen, and fearing that she might be the cause of a terrible war, they were planning to stone her to death as soon as she entered the city.

But when Helen walked through the gates, all the men, as they looked down at her, saw their own most secret longings, their deepest desires, reflected back to themselves. All the women were enchanted by her beauty. All the children fell in love with her. They dropped the rocks and stones they were carrying.

And it was not only the people of Troy who fell in love with Helen. All the horses of the city fell for her as well. All the dogs and cats, all the pigeons perched on the gutters, even the stones

of the city turned toward her in a strange, crystalline way, as iron filings might turn toward a lodestone.

King Priam, the white-bearded father of Troy, swore a solemn oath by all the mighty gods and goddesses that no one would ever take Helen away.

Across the sea there came a thousand ships. Each ship was crammed with warriors, with flashing breastplates and plumed helmets. One morning a warrior at the front of the first ship blew a bronze trumpet. The men behind him stood and stared. They saw what he had seen. They saw a broad beach of white sand. Behind the beach was a fertile plain, with fields and farms, vineyards and shambling cattle. Two rivers ran on either side of the plain. Beyond both rivers, the Greeks saw long ridges leading to headlands that overlooked the sea.

And at the back of the plain they saw a city wrapped in stone, a tremendous city bristling with turrets and towers. The walls were as tall and broad as any they'd ever seen. Behind the city a mountain rose into cloud.

The men who saw that sight felt a tingling in their bellies, a mingling of excitement and terror. Surely some god or goddess must have had a hand in the building of such a place. Surely one of them must watch over it.

Perhaps this was the dwelling place of the gods and goddesses themselves.

From the high walls of Troy, from the turrets and the towers, the people of the city saw a darkening on the horizon where the sea met the sky. They rubbed their eyes and looked again. Now they could see a thousand flecks of mast, each with its colored rag of sail. They rubbed their eyes again and they could see a thousand ships slicing toward them through the waves. Each ship was crammed with warriors.

The Trojans wasted no time. There was a greasing of axles and a harnessing of horses to chariots. There was a sharpening of swords and a seizing of helmets and shields. There was a buckling of breastplates, belts and greaves.

The bronze Scaean gates of the city were thrown open and the Trojan army poured across the plain with a whirring of wheels, a creaking of chariots, a neighing of horses, a shouting of men and a thundering of hooves and feet. With a crash of bronze against bronze, the Trojans met the Greeks as they waded ashore from their ships.

Striding among the Trojans was a warrior called Cygnus. He stood head and shoulders above all other men. His skin was charmed against the striking of all weapons: sword, dagger, spear, arrow, battle-ax. He was a son of Poseidon, the god

of the sea. He was white-skinned, white-lipped, white-tongued, as white as sea foam, as white as the seventh wave of the sea.

He cut down Greeks with every stroke of his sword, with every thrust of his spear, while Greek swords buckled against his skin and Greek spears glanced from him as if glancing from stone. He left a wake of dead behind himself as he fought.

Achilles's ship had yet to yield her cargo. From his ship, Achilles watched, his heart in turmoil. He watched the savage Cygnus cutting a path through the Greek ranks, like a plough through moist earth.

Tethered to the mast of Achilles's ship were the four white horses that once had been the crests of waves. They had been given to Achilles's parents on their wedding day by the god of the sea, Poseidon. Sometimes they would speak. Now one of them – Beauty was his name – lifted his long head and said,

"Son of Peleus, you know the fate that looms over you. You know that if you set foot on these shores and join this war, yours will be a short life. Not for you the stretching shadows, not for you the ripening grape, not for you the joy of children. You are matchless on the field of battle. No man could ever harm you. But a god could."

Achilles replied, "My dear horse, you speak so rarely, and yet you waste your words. I choose death, so that my name will live forever on the tongues of men and women!"

And with a cry, he drew his sword, stabbed the air and leapt from the ship.

The Trojans watched Achilles flying through the air like a dancer. They saw his foot strike the white sand. A spring of fresh water burst out of the ground where he landed. They watched him run across the battlefield as though he was running through long grass.

When he drew close to Cygnus he lifted the spear that could draw blood from the wind.

"Know it was Achilles who killed you," he said.

With all the strength of his arm he hurled his spear. It struck Cygnus's throat and clattered down to the ground at his feet as though it was a reed that had been thrown by a little boy. Cygnus lifted both his arms and laughed.

"Throw another one, my little friend. I know who you are. You're Thetis's son, but I'm no more afraid of you than of a mosquito that I might smear across my arm.

From head to foot my skin is charmed against the striking of all weapons."

Achilles drew his bronze sword and attacked Cygnus. He leapt and twisted, cutting and slashing with his sharp-edged blade until Cygnus's armor hung from his body like a shattered eggshell. But still the white skin was unscratched, and still Cygnus laughed at Achilles. Then he lifted his spear and threw it. He threw it with such force that Achilles staggered backward. The blade had penetrated the gold of the shield. It had penetrated nine layers of hardened oxhide.

But then Achilles caught his balance and smiled grimly. It was as though, in that moment, he'd solved a riddle. His lips stretched back from his teeth and he screamed. He leapt and smashed his shield into Cygnus's face. He ground the boss of the shield to the left and the right, until Cygnus's nose was smeared across his cheek and his teeth were shattered.

Cygnus fell backward and Achilles knelt on his shoulders. He tore the helmet from Cygnus's head and wrapped the helmet straps around his throat. He tugged and twisted and tightened the tourniquet until Cygnus's head was half torn from his shoulders and every last shudder of life was gone from him.

Then a strange thing happened. The twisted, broken neck of Cygnus began to stretch and to curve. His face narrowed. His mouth stretched and hardened into a beak. White feathers pushed through his white skin. His father Poseidon had taken pity on him and had transformed him into a swan.

Cygnus beat his feathered arms against the air and the shattered eggshell armor fell from his body. He flew up and up into the sky, high above the battlefield. Every warrior stared up at him. There was no sound but the sighing and the soughing of his wings.

Three times he circled above both armies, then he flew over the white sands, over the masts of the ships, over the blue waves and he was gone.

As soon as Cygnus was out of sight, Achilles lifted his sword, threw back his head and roared with fury. Fearlessly he leapt and bounded across the plain toward the Trojan army with his black Myrmidons close behind him.

The blood in the heart of every Trojan thinned to water. They turned tail, galloping and running headlong back to the city. They fled before Achilles. They retreated to the safety of Troy and the great bronze Scaean gates were slammed shut behind them.

And from that day onward, to every Trojan warrior, the very sound of Achilles's name was like a cold shudder from the nape of the neck to the root of the spine.

The Greeks let loose a scattering of lazy arrows after the retreating Trojans and then turned and made their way back down to the seashore. They set about dragging their high-prowed ships up onto the white sand.

They set them in rows, one behind the other. Beside each ship they built huts of wood and reeds and mounded earth. Around the ships they built a high wall, a palisade. Great gates were built and hung. A deep trench was dug between the two rivers.

This was a camp as big as a city. Every region of Greece had its own district of the camp, its own shops and stables and smithies, streets and secret alleys, exercise areas and burial places. In the center of the camp was an open area, an agora, where debates were held, where altars to the immortals, the undying gods, were built.

In front of the camp could be seen the fields, the farms, the vineyards, the cattle grazing all unknowing. It was four hours' walk between the Greek camp and Troy.

From high on the ramparts, from the walls and turrets and towers of the city, the Trojans watched the Greek army. They watched the building of the camp. They watched the digging of the trench from the River Scamander to the River Xanthus. They watched the lifting of the wooden palisade. They watched the smoke of tens of thousands of campfires drifting up into the sky.

And they watched the swarming Greeks themselves, like flies around the cowsheds in the spring when the pails are creamy-white with milk, busy about their business.

Then one morning, as dawn took her golden throne, the Trojans saw the wooden gates of the palisade, the high fence around the Greek camp, swing open. Tens, hundreds, thousands of Greek warriors, foot soldiers and charioteers, rank upon rank, file upon file, came pouring out of the camp.

They took their places across the plain. Every man had a bronze helmet, a bronze breastplate, a bronze shield on his arm and a bronze sword at his belt. Every man was staring at the city with slaughter in his heart.

And the Trojans watched the Greek kings, striding amongst the ranks and files like stallions moving among the mares and foals of a huge herd of horses.

The Trojan army wasted no time. The Scaean gates were thrown open and they took their positions before the city walls.

Then the two armies fell upon one another with a deafening, clattering clamor of bronze against bronze. As two rivers in full spate, each carrying a flotsam of uprooted trees might crash and collide, so the Trojans and the Greeks met upon the field of battle.

But Achilles and his matchless Myrmidons attacked with such savage ferocity that the Trojans were soon driven back against the stone walls of their city. And then, in turn, from the high turrets and towers and parapets, a black rain of Trojan arrows drove the Greeks back toward their ships.

This was a pattern that was to repeat itself over and over again. In battle after battle the Greeks were unbeatable on the open plain. Achilles was unstoppable. He was like an unquenchable fire. But as soon as the Trojans retreated to the city walls the Greeks could do no more. They could not withstand the relentless showers of sharp arrows, and they could not break down the stone walls.

King Priam and his eldest son, Prince Hector, decided that patience was the best strategy. Their city was their strongest shield. They ordered the people of Troy to stay inside the city walls. If they waited long enough the Greeks would give up and sail home. There was no need for any more bloodshed. And there were plenty of secret tunnels and hidden entrances off Mount Ida by which their allies could bring them food.

So it was that the siege of Troy began.

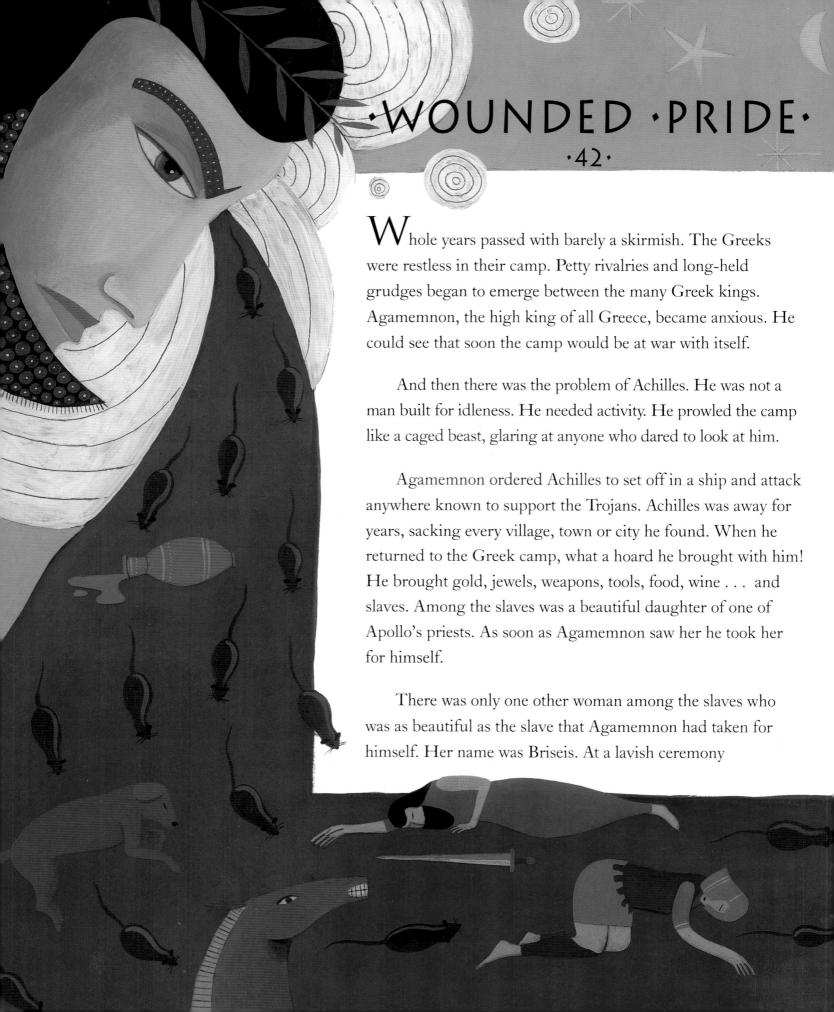

Whole years passed with barely a skirmish. The Greeks were restless in their camp. Petty rivalries and long-held grudges began to emerge between the many Greek kings. Agamemnon, the high king of all Greece, became anxious. He could see that soon the camp would be at war with itself.

And then there was the problem of Achilles. He was not a man built for idleness. He needed activity. He prowled the camp like a caged beast, glaring at anyone who dared to look at him.

Agamemnon ordered Achilles to set off in a ship and attack anywhere known to support the Trojans. Achilles was away for years, sacking every village, town or city he found. When he returned to the Greek camp, what a hoard he brought with him! He brought gold, jewels, weapons, tools, food, wine . . . and slaves. Among the slaves was a beautiful daughter of one of Apollo's priests. As soon as Agamemnon saw her he took her for himself.

There was only one other woman among the slaves who was as beautiful as the slave that Agamemnon had taken for himself. Her name was Briseis. At a lavish ceremony

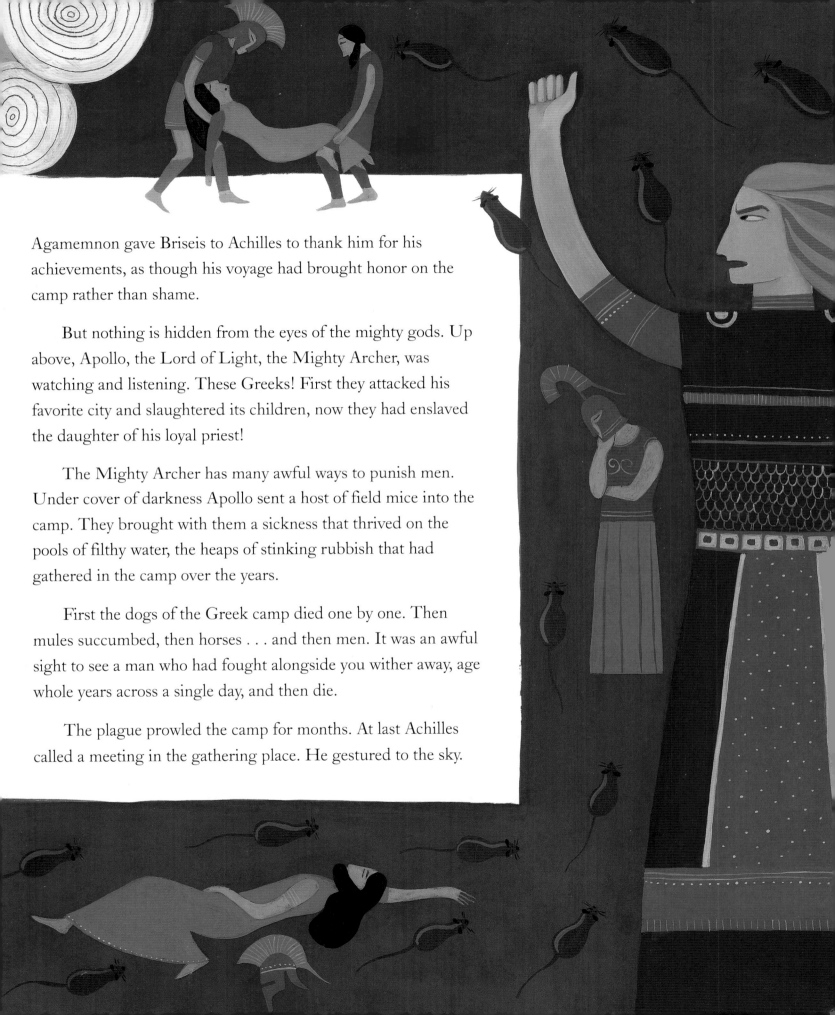

Agamemnon gave Briseis to Achilles to thank him for his achievements, as though his voyage had brought honor on the camp rather than shame.

But nothing is hidden from the eyes of the mighty gods. Up above, Apollo, the Lord of Light, the Mighty Archer, was watching and listening. These Greeks! First they attacked his favorite city and slaughtered its children, now they had enslaved the daughter of his loyal priest!

The Mighty Archer has many awful ways to punish men. Under cover of darkness Apollo sent a host of field mice into the camp. They brought with them a sickness that thrived on the pools of filthy water, the heaps of stinking rubbish that had gathered in the camp over the years.

First the dogs of the Greek camp died one by one. Then mules succumbed, then horses . . . and then men. It was an awful sight to see a man who had fought alongside you wither away, age whole years across a single day, and then die.

The plague prowled the camp for months. At last Achilles called a meeting in the gathering place. He gestured to the sky.

"Wherever I turn my head I can see the smoke of funeral pyres. Something must be done! There is one among us who can understand the moods of the immortals by the patterns the birds make as they fly. We have a prophet, a seer, a wise man. Why does Calchas not help us?"

Calchas winced.

"Great Achilles," he said, "before I speak, promise me your protection. The bearer of bad news is never welcome. My words will bring upon me the anger of the powerful."

Achilles bowed his head. Calchas continued.

"This plague has been sent by Apollo. The Lord of Light, the Mighty Archer, is furious with us because our high king has taken to his bed a daughter of Apollo's loyal priest. Until that woman is set free, every day will see more dead."

Agamemnon sighed.

"Old man, would good news burn your tongue? I feed you and clothe you, and yet you never give me a single word of encouragement in return! Every time you open your mouth, another humiliation is heaped upon me. I love this woman, as dearly as I love my wife, Clytemnestra, so far away! But since I value the well-being of my subjects more than I do my own peace of mind, I'll let her go tomorrow – with gold. But that means that I, your high king, am to receive nothing from the spoils of Achilles's voyage.

That is unthinkable! If I am to give up this woman, I want another one instead."

"From where?" said Achilles. "There are no slaves left to be shared out. Surely you of all of us know that! When Troy falls things will be different; your loss will be made up three or four times over."

"Thank you," said Agamemnon. "But I seem to remember that I am the high king, not you. You are just some prince under my command. But since you are so keen to make up my loss, I'll take a woman from you. Yes, that Briseis, whom I gave you when you first returned from your voyage. She is mine now!"

Achilles took a step forward. He felt a hand on his shoulder. He turned and saw his friend Patroclus shaking his head. Achilles stepped back.

Had it not been for that gentle hand, Achilles would have beaten the high king to the ground.

"Take her," said Achilles. "But this means I will not fight for you again. No oath binds me to the protection of Helen. I was not one of those kings who stood on the severed limbs of a stallion and swore to protect her all those years ago. And yet I have fought for you. For what? So that when finally I find a woman whom I cherish, you can take her from me?

"I will not fight for you again, not if you beg me!"

"Good!" said Agamemnon. "Go! The lowliest soldier in the shabbiest squad in this army knows that to win this war he must obey his king. You are not a warrior; you are a monster. Never have I seen such delight in the eyes of one when he took the life of another. This camp is better off without you!"

Agamemnon turned on his heel and stormed off before another word could be spoken. The crowd dispersed, leaving only Achilles and Patroclus in the gathering place. Achilles was shaking with fury.

The next day Agamemnon set free the daughter of Apollo's priest. She sailed home in one of the high king's ships. As soon as she set foot on her homeland, the plague in the Greek camp ended. Apollo turned his awful glare elsewhere.

And two soldiers were sent across the Greek camp, down to where the breakers crashed and dragged, to the hut of Achilles. They were terrified as they approached his

hut, but he greeted them politely and yielded Briseis immediately, though they saw tears in his eyes as they parted.

That night, when the sky was bright with stars, Achilles walked down to the edge of the sea. He waded into the shallows. His face creased into a childish sob. Through his tears he saw the shining path made by the moon. Down that path walked his mother, Thetis.

"Mother, many a time I heard you boast that Zeus longs for you and lusts after you. Go to him now. He could make these Greeks taste pain. I want blood in the sand. I want the ships of this camp burning. Then they will remember that I was out on the battlefield, severing heads with every stroke of my sword, while their fawn-hearted, dog-faced king cowered behind the palisade!"

"My son," she said, "I can refuse you nothing. I will go to Zeus, whose temple is the sky. Until then, stay by the ships."

47

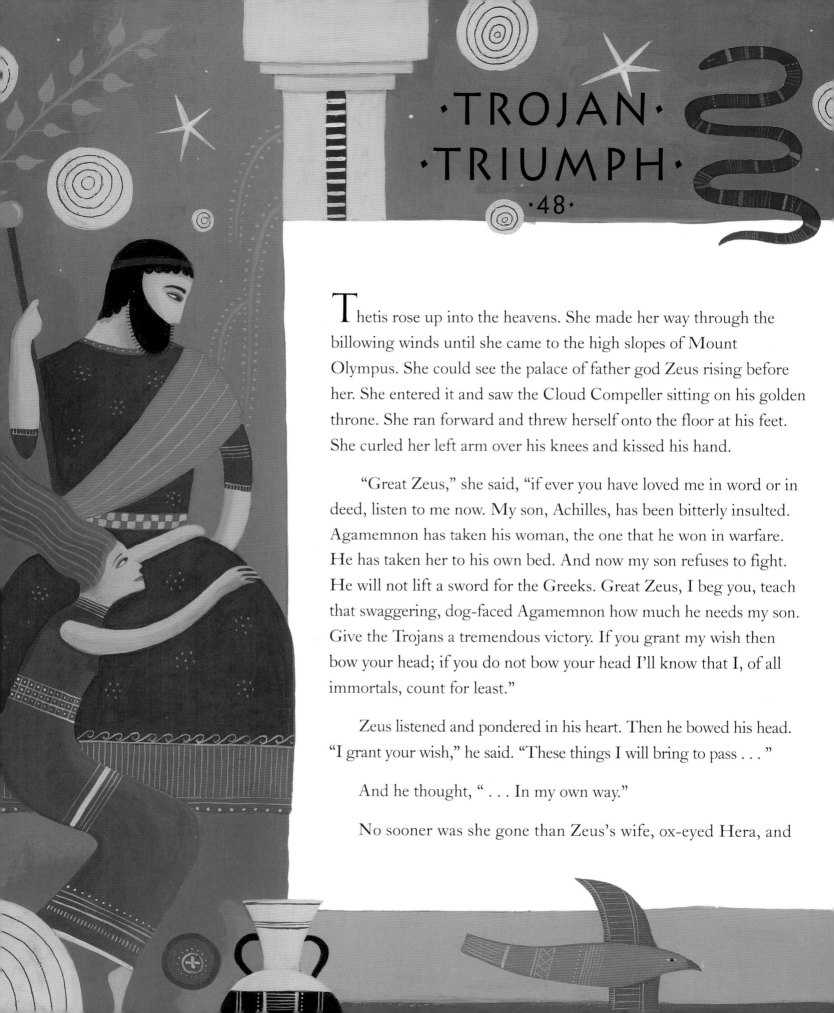

Thetis rose up into the heavens. She made her way through the billowing winds until she came to the high slopes of Mount Olympus. She could see the palace of father god Zeus rising before her. She entered it and saw the Cloud Compeller sitting on his golden throne. She ran forward and threw herself onto the floor at his feet. She curled her left arm over his knees and kissed his hand.

"Great Zeus," she said, "if ever you have loved me in word or in deed, listen to me now. My son, Achilles, has been bitterly insulted. Agamemnon has taken his woman, the one that he won in warfare. He has taken her to his own bed. And now my son refuses to fight. He will not lift a sword for the Greeks. Great Zeus, I beg you, teach that swaggering, dog-faced Agamemnon how much he needs my son. Give the Trojans a tremendous victory. If you grant my wish then bow your head; if you do not bow your head I'll know that I, of all immortals, count for least."

Zeus listened and pondered in his heart. Then he bowed his head. "I grant your wish," he said. "These things I will bring to pass . . ."

And he thought, " . . . In my own way."

No sooner was she gone than Zeus's wife, ox-eyed Hera, and

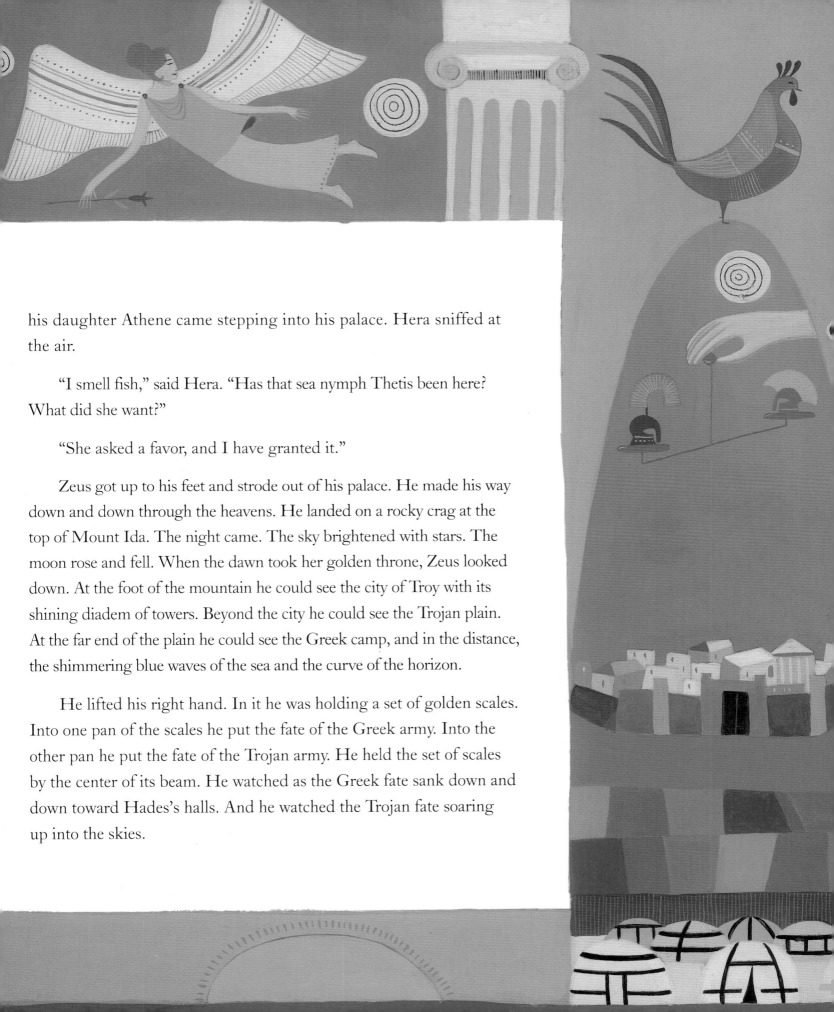

his daughter Athene came stepping into his palace. Hera sniffed at the air.

"I smell fish," said Hera. "Has that sea nymph Thetis been here? What did she want?"

"She asked a favor, and I have granted it."

Zeus got up to his feet and strode out of his palace. He made his way down and down through the heavens. He landed on a rocky crag at the top of Mount Ida. The night came. The sky brightened with stars. The moon rose and fell. When the dawn took her golden throne, Zeus looked down. At the foot of the mountain he could see the city of Troy with its shining diadem of towers. Beyond the city he could see the Trojan plain. At the far end of the plain he could see the Greek camp, and in the distance, the shimmering blue waves of the sea and the curve of the horizon.

He lifted his right hand. In it he was holding a set of golden scales. Into one pan of the scales he put the fate of the Greek army. Into the other pan he put the fate of the Trojan army. He held the set of scales by the center of its beam. He watched as the Greek fate sank down and down toward Hades's halls. And he watched the Trojan fate soaring up into the skies.

At that very moment, in the city of Troy, Prince Hector woke with a sudden courage soaring in his breast. The eldest son of King Priam leapt out of bed. He kissed his wife, Andromache, who was still sleeping. He pulled on his clothes and his armor. He strode out of his palace and sent lieutenants to all corners of the city to wake warriors.

Soon the air was thick with the sound of the greasing of axles and the harnessing of horses, with the sharpening of swords and the seizing of helmets and shields, with the buckling of breastplates, belts and greaves. And Hector himself, with the leather rim of his bossed shield tapping the nape of his neck and the backs of his ankles, strode the length and breadth of Troy, exhorting and encouraging his men.

When the whole city was humming Hector made his way to the palace of his brother, Prince Paris. He climbed the stairs and pushed open the door of Paris's bedchamber. Paris was still in bed. He was leaning against his soft pillows and rubbing scented oils into the wood of his bow. Helen was lying beside him.

"Paris, get out of bed!" said Hector. "What must our Trojan warriors think, who every day defend the city for your sake, while you rarely venture out of your bedchamber?"

Helen climbed out of bed. She took Hector's hand and kissed it.

"Sweet Hector, of all the children of Priam you bear the greatest burden, and all because of Paris and me, foolish, love-struck mooncalves that we are, tormented by the

heavens and destined to live on in the tales and songs of men and women yet unborn. Hector, sit down, stretch out your legs, have a cup of wine."

"Helen," said Hector. "I have no time for wine! Get this man out of bed! Paris, I'll meet you at the Scaean gates!"

Hector ran out of his brother's palace and hurried through the city streets. As he passed his own palace he saw his wife, Andromache, walking swiftly toward him.

Behind her a servant followed, holding their son, Astyanax, in her arms. Andromache's cheeks were wet with tears. She threw her arms around Hector's neck.

"Hector, this sudden courage will be the death of you. Achilles is a wild animal. He is a savage beast. In his ravaging the coast from the Black Sea to the Nile he has killed all seven of my brothers. He has killed my father and my mother. He has reduced my birthplace to a heap of blackened rubble. Hector, do not make me a widow as well as an orphan."

Hector shook his head.

"Andromache, what am I to do? If a shepherd is guarding his flocks on the slopes of Mount Ida and he finds himself surrounded by wolves or thieves, does he turn tail and run or does he stand firm and fight? I am my father's son. I am our son's father. This land from Mount Ida to the sea, from the River Scamander to the River Xanthus is my inheritance. I must fight: to protect you and to protect our land."

She looked up at him.

"Then whom are you married to? Me or the land?"

He kissed the top of her head.

"Both, my love."

Then he reached forward and took his son from the servant's arms. Astyanax opened his mouth and screamed. Tears spurted out of his eyes. Andromache smiled through her tears.

"Sweet Hector, it is your helmet that frightens him."

She reached up and lifted the bronze helmet with its nodding horsehair plume from Hector's head. She set it down on the ground. Hector lifted his son. He rubbed his nose against the baby's nose. The tears turned into gurgling, bubbling laughter. He lifted Astyanax high above his head.

"Great Father Zeus. May this child grow up to be greater than his father."

The Cloud Compeller looked down from the rocky crag on Mount Ida. He smiled fondly, but he did not bow his head in assent.

Hector passed the baby to Andromache. He picked up his helmet and put it onto his head.

"Andromache, no one, whether hero or coward, can avoid his fate."

He turned and made his way down toward the Scaean gates.

It was at that moment that Prince Paris appeared. He was wearing a leopard-skin cloak over his shoulders. His polished bow was slung across his back. As a great hillocky bull that's been kept inside all winter will skip and dance across the flowery meadows when the barn doors are thrown open in the spring, so Paris came jauntily stepping down the city street. Hector threw his arm around his brother's neck and kissed him.

Then Hector approached his golden chariot. It stood waiting at the gates. His two horses had already been harnessed to it. They were stamping and steaming and chomping at their bits. Hector stroked their faces with the back of his hand.

"My beauties, today is your chance to repay me for all those mornings when my wife, Andromache, gave you honeyed wheat before she brought me my own breakfast."

Then he climbed up into the car of his chariot and faced the huge Trojan army that was massing inside the city walls.

"My friends, today we ride against the Greeks," said Hector. "Great Zeus is on our side. I feel it in my bones. We will drive them before us. When we reach their flimsy, futile palisade our horses' hooves will kick it down. And when we reach their hollow ships the watchword will be FIRE!"

There was a tremendous cheer from the Trojan army. The city gates were thrown open and they poured across the plain with a whirring of wheels, a creaking of chariots, a neighing of horses, a shouting of men and a thundering of hooves and feet. With a crash of bronze against bronze, the Trojans met the Greeks.

Paris was in the thick of the battle, his cloak billowing behind him, fierce among his foes. Old Priam swung his sword, hungry for blood.

And Hector led the way as his charioteer whipped his horses to a gallop. Every cell of his body was poised, immaculate. He killed Greeks with every stroke of his sword, with every thrust of his spear. He cut down Greeks like ripe corn, leaving them in swathes six-deep behind him.

Behind King Priam and his two sons the Trojan army followed. They drove the Greeks before them. They drove them back to the wooden palisade. The Trojan horses kicked it down like little boys on the seashore kicking down sand castles.

The Trojans clambered over the shattered wooden walls and entered the Greek camp.

Every Greek heart turned to water. They fled before the Trojans.

Hector hunted them down. There was menace in his eyes as they flickered beneath the bronze rim of his helmet. There was menace in the tilt of his helmet as he fought.

Behind Hector, through the breach in the palisade, there came a surge of brazen Trojan warriors, each one brandishing a flaming torch. They kicked over the burial mounds. They threw spears at fleeing Greek backs. They gutted the wounded Greeks who could not flee.

The Greeks formed a line before their ships. They fought with whatever they could find: axes, sticks, even rocks. Menelaus climbed aboard one of them and swung an oar, cracking Trojan heads with every stroke . . . but soon black smoke began to rise into the sky. The Greek ships were on fire.

Across the camp, where the breakers crashed and dragged, Achilles listened to the sound of the burning ships, he listened to the sound of the dying Greeks, then he picked up a silver lyre and sang a song of the deeds of heroes.

·PATROCLUS·
·57·

On the high slopes of Mount Olympus two goddesses, ox-eyed Hera and owl-eyed Athene, sat and watched the smoke rising from the Greek ships. The blood drained from their faces. This was terrible. The Trojans were victorious. Something would have to be done. This called for desperate measures.

Hera jumped to her feet and ran to her palace. She locked all the doors. She washed herself from head to foot. She rubbed scented oils into her skin. She threw a beautiful shimmering robe over her shoulders and clasped it with a golden brooch. Then she unlocked the doors and searched Olympus until she found the goddess of love. She smiled.

"Aphrodite, dear child, I wonder if you would do me a favor, if you're not too angry with me for siding with the Greeks."

Aphrodite looked at her.

"What favor?"

"I wonder if you'd be kind enough to lend me your girdle of love and desire? You see, the sky and the earth have fallen out with one another. They do nothing but bicker and quarrel. If I could borrow your girdle perhaps I could make peace between them."

"Well," said Aphrodite. "It would be churlish of me not to lend you my girdle for such an important task."

Aphrodite unfastened the girdle and handed it across to Hera. She took it, nodded her thanks and walked away. As soon as she was out of sight, Hera tied the girdle around her own waist. Then she flew downward. She descended through the skies, down and down to the rocky crag on Mount Ida where Zeus was watching the destruction of the Greek ships. She sat down beside him. Suddenly Zeus turned to her and smiled.

"Hera! Never have I been filled with such sweet desire, such tender longing for mortal or immortal."

He seized her hand and kissed it.

"Not even when I held Leda in my arms, or Leto, or the incomparable daughter of Phoenix, or Demeter, or Semele, or Thetis . . . "

Hera blushed with false modesty.

"But Zeus, we might be seen. Think how gossiping tongues would wag."

"Don't worry my love," said Zeus, "I'll cover us with a golden cloud."

He brought down a cloud that dripped golden dew onto the ground, and they lay on the mountaintop together and took their delight of one another. But like all wives Hera knew her husband's habits. She knew that it wouldn't be long before he fell asleep in her arms. Soon he was snoring and snorting like a pig in clover. She gently laid him on his side.

Hera jumped to her feet, threw the shimmering robe over her shoulders and swooped down to the Greek camp. She shrouded herself in invisibility and moved

among the terrified Greek warriors until she found Patroclus. And when she found him, she filled him with sudden, tremendous courage.

Patroclus ran through the screams and smoke, down to where the breakers crashed and dragged.

He burst into Achilles's hut. Achilles was strumming a lyre as though this day were like any other.

"Achilles, the ships are on fire! Menelaus, Odysseus, Agamemnon, all of them have been wounded! If you will not fight today, lend me your armor. You know the very sight of it will put the Trojans to flight!"

So this was how Patroclus brought upon himself his own death.

"Very well!" said Achilles. "Wear my armor, lead my army, and ride in my chariot. You can be Achilles today. Drive the Trojans from the camp – but be careful. Apollo loves Troy. If you put the city in any danger, he will punish you, and his punishments are awful and swift."

And so for the first time Patroclus strapped on Achilles's well-made greaves, and the golden breastplate emblazoned with silver stars. He put on Achilles's helmet, its black horsehair plume bristling with terror.

Then Patroclus took off the wonderful ring, the ring Achilles had given him years before, the ring cast in the shape of a curling arrow whose sharp point touched its feathered tail.

"You have entrusted your armor to me. Take this, until my return."

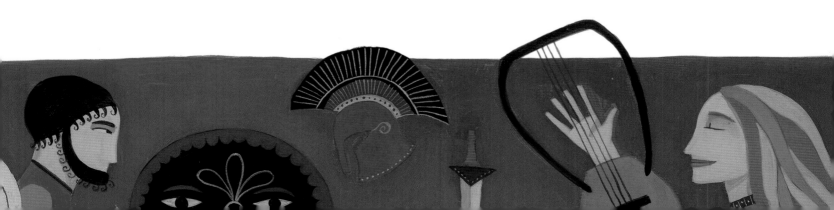

Achilles smiled. He slipped the ring onto his finger.

Patroclus climbed into the car of Achilles's chariot and he set forth.

Suddenly the Trojans, as they were torching the Greek ships, saw Achilles. They saw Achilles in his golden breastplate emblazoned with silver stars. They saw Achilles with his matchless Myrmidons. Every man felt a cold shudder from the nape of the neck to the root of the spine. They dropped their torches. They scattered in all directions. No word of Hector's would rally them. They scrambled over the shattered palisade. They escaped to save their own skins.

Death rode a chariot that day. Patroclus and the Myrmidons fastened on the Trojans, as when a little boy hears a strange sound from inside a hollow tree, he picks up a stick and jabs the shadows, and the wasps that are nesting inside come swarming out and attack him, a seething black cloud of frenzied rage. So the Myrmidons fell upon their enemies. The Trojans tumbled to the ground with jolting groans, with splintered teeth and shattered bones. Like a hawk swooping from the sky into a flock of starlings, Patroclus drove them across the battlefield, until he saw the walls of Troy rise before him, until he saw man-slaying Hector flee before his charge.

Patroclus . . . did you forget?

Did the blur of battle muddle your mind?

Or did you decide to try the last despite Achilles's warning?

You went too far.

High on the rocky crag Zeus woke up. He stretched. He yawned. He smiled to himself and glanced down from Mount Ida. The Trojan army was in full retreat.

He leapt to his feet. He thundered with fury.

He could see Patroclus, dressed in Achilles's armor, driving the Trojans back toward the city. Behind Patroclus he could see the Myrmidons, and behind the Myrmidons the whole Greek army. He could see his wife, Hera, and his daughter Athene striding invisibly among the Greeks, urging them forward. Trembling with anger he threw back his head and bellowed.

"HERA!"

The goddess stopped and looked upward. She would have been completely destroyed by the lightning-flash ferocity of Zeus's gaze had she not still been wearing Aphrodite's girdle of love and desire, which softened his heart toward her.

"Hera! Athene! Go to Olympus now! And send me Apollo!"

The two goddesses, shaking and quaking with terror, fled into the sky.

Soon golden Apollo, the founder of the city, was standing in front of Zeus.

"Apollo. Go to Troy and help Hector all you can."

Trojan-loving Apollo wasted no time. As swift as thought, he flew into the city. Hector was on the battlements, in the thick of the fighting. Three times Patroclus, dressed in Achilles's armor, had clambered almost to the summit of the city walls.

Three times he'd been driven back by Trojan spears.

As Hector fought he heard a voice beside him:

"Hector!"

Hector turned. There was a warrior standing beside him whom he'd never seen before.

"Hector, why do you stay inside the city walls? Why do you not go out and fight the golden-armored one? Who knows, perhaps Apollo would help you."

The warrior vanished and there was a golden light hanging in the air where he had been standing. Hector was filled with spirit and awe in the certain knowledge that he had been in the presence of one of the immortal gods. He ran down the stone steps. He leapt into the car of his chariot. His charioteer whipped the horses to a gallop.

The bronze Scaean gates of the city were thrown open. Hector rode out of Troy.

Across the plain in the Greek camp, Achilles was pacing by the gates, waiting for Patroclus to return. Suddenly, a thousand Trojan voices cried out for joy and the air was filled with a tremendous shout.

Achilles's hand was wet and sticky. He lifted it to his face. The ring that Patroclus had given him for safekeeping, the ring cast in the shape of a curling arrow whose sharp point touched its feathered tail, that golden ring was weeping blood. Blood trickled down the back of his hand and dropped from his elbow into the mud. Achilles shuddered.

It was Odysseus who made his way from the battlefield to break the terrible news. Patroclus had been killed by man-slaying Hector. Odysseus opened the door of the hut. Achilles was on his hands and knees, shaking. His clothes had been ripped to rags. In his fists were clumps of his own hair that he had wrenched from his head. His eyes were red, bloodshot, bulging. He ground his teeth, and then he threw back his head and let loose such a howl of fury and sorrow that Odysseus fled. The scream echoed into the depths of the ocean. Thetis heard it. She came at once.

Achilles was trembling as she approached him.

"Mother!" he said, "Patroclus has been slaughtered. Hector killed him, and stripped my burnished armor from his back! Before my time is over I'll kill Hector with my bare hands! I will fight him without armor! I will fight him naked if need be!"

"My son," said Thetis, "I'll win you armor. Promise me you will not go into battle until I return!"

And she was gone.

Thetis flew up into the heavens. She came to the high slopes of Mount Olympus. She hurried between the palaces of the immortals until she reached the workshop of Hephaestos, the crippled god of metalwork. She pushed open the door. The hunchbacked god was shaping a golden tripod. In one hand he was holding a hammer, in the other a pair of tongs. When he saw her he smiled. He put down his tools and wiped his hands on a dripping sponge.

"Thetis! What brings you here?"

Her face was crumpled with sorrow.

"Patroclus has been killed," she said. "Man-slaying Hector has killed him, and he has torn my son Achilles's armor from Patroclus's back. Achilles has been left with no armor to wear. Hephaestos, I beg you, make him a new suit of armor."

Hephaestos put his hand gently on her shoulder.

"I wish I could make him armor that would protect him from his fate. But I can make him a suit of armor that will fill his heart with joy, and will fill the eyes of all mortals with wonder."

He put tin and bronze and gold and silver into melting vats and he began to fashion a magnificent suit of armor. He made beautiful greaves of pliant tin. He made a breastplate of bronze that shone like the sun. He made a golden helmet with a golden plume and golden tassels.

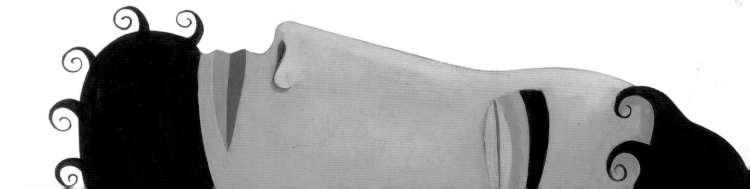

And he made a great shield. On it he wrought the earth and the sky, with the sun and the moon and all the constellations. He divided the earth into two kingdoms. One was at peace, with a spiraling wedding dance, a trickling stream, clusters of purple grapes and shambling cattle grazing on sweet grass. The other was at war, with a city under siege, and all the terrible tumult of the battlefield.

When the precious pieces were finished he gave them to Thetis. She seized them from his hands, thanked him with all of her heart and descended from the heavens.

The corpse of Patroclus was brought to Achilles. He laid it on a fur. All night he sat beside it, murmuring, rocking. Next morning his mother descended with glorious armor. She laid it before him piece by piece.

Achilles sighed. He stood. He scraped the tears from his cheeks with the heel of his hand. He strapped on the greaves of pliant tin, the bronze breastplate, the golden helmet with golden tassels and a golden plume. Each piece was shaped to perfection, cool against his skin. He felt lighter with them on, as though he wore invisible wings. He took a sword. He picked up the marvelous shield that lit up the sky like the moon. He climbed into the car of his chariot. Before him were his four white horses: Lightfoot, Beauty, Dapple and Dancer. He spoke.

"This time, bring your master home."

"Yes," said Beauty. "We'll save your life today. But do not blame us for the death of Patroclus. It was a god who killed him, and the mighty gods will kill you too."

"What would you have me do? Cower in my hut while Hector struts in my father's bronze? If I am meant to die here, far from my father and mother, then so be it. But before I die, I'll see the Trojans have their glut of war!"

And he was out of the camp then, among his enemies, like inhuman fire raging in the mountains, like a mountain lion, like the god of battle. He fought until the ground was sticky with blood. Eyes blazing, teeth bared, heart pounding, scorning fear, the headlong runner, ablaze with fury, too bright to look at, hacked a path toward the city.

All the Trojans fled before Achilles. They ran back to the city and the Scaean gates were closed behind them. Every Trojan warrior fled except for Hector. He stood outside the city walls. He was dressed in Achilles's armor. The golden breastplate emblazoned with silver stars glittered in the fierce sun. He watched and waited. Above him white-bearded Priam leaned over the parapet to call to him.

"Hector, my son, come inside. Or have the mighty gods and goddesses condemned me to linger on the outermost rim of old age, suffering intolerable grief?"

Queen Hecuba and Andromache, with little Astyanax in her arms, beckoned to him.

"Come inside!"

But he turned his back resolutely on them all. He was searching in all directions with his eyes. He was searching the jostling sea of Greek helmets. Suddenly he saw what he was looking for. Among the bronze helmets with their horsehair plumes he caught a glimpse of a golden one, with a golden plume and golden tassels. He saw Achilles.

And in the same instant Achilles saw Hector. He leapt from his chariot like a dancer. He bounded across the battlefield, vaulting shattered chariots, jumping over corpses and horses.

As he drew closer Hector could see that Achilles's shining armor was dripping with blood and gore. As he drew closer still he could see that Achilles's mouth was open, and from his throat he heard a terrible screaming, screeching, piercing cry of grief and fury.

Hector looked down at the earth beneath his feet. He looked up at his father, his mother, his son, his wife, and in that moment he knew that he wanted life. He wanted life more than any glorious death on the battlefield. He turned and ran. He knew every hill and hollow, every ridge and contour of this land. He ran like a deer.

And Achilles pursued him. He tracked him like a dog. He followed every twist and turn. Three times Hector ran around the city walls with Achilles close behind him.

High on his rocky crag on Mount Ida, great Zeus the Cloud Compeller was watching Hector and Achilles. In his right hand he was holding the set of golden scales.

Into one pan of the scales he put the fate of Hector. Into the other pan he put the fate of Achilles. He held the set of scales by the center of its beam. He watched as Hector's fate sank down and down toward Hades's halls. And he watched as Achilles's fate soared up into the skies.

And in that moment, all the immortal gods and goddesses deserted Hector.

Owl-eyed Athene swooped down from the heavens and stood outside the city walls. She changed her shape so that to all the world she looked like Paris. And as Hector ran headlong toward her, with Achilles close behind, she called out in Paris's voice.

"Hector! Hector!"

Hector stopped and turned.

"Paris! You alone have ventured through the city gates and I love you for it."

"Hector, why don't we make a stand against Achilles, you and I together?"

Hector nodded. He turned and faced the swift runner. Achilles stopped dead. He curled his lips back from his teeth and screamed. He lifted his spear and hurled it at Hector with all the strength of his arm. Hector dodged to one side and the spear lodged quivering in the ground behind him. Hector lifted his own spear. But he did not see his brother disappear. He did not see the goddess, invisible, lifting Achilles's spear into the air. He hurled his spear at Achilles. It struck his shield and glanced to one side. Hector turned to Paris.

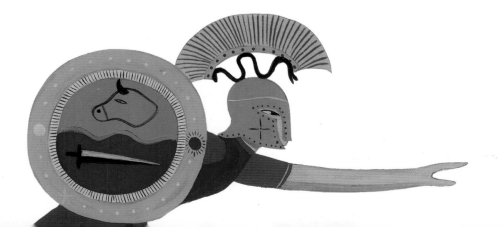

"My brother, give me Achilles's spear . . . "

But Paris had vanished. He turned again and saw that Achilles was holding his own spear once more. And in that moment he understood that he had been tricked by one of the immortals. He drew his sword and ran toward Achilles. He could see his own reflection in Achilles's breastplate.

But already Achilles's spear, that could draw blood from the wind, was singing through the air. It struck Hector in the throat. It jutted through the nape of his neck. He dropped to his knees. The hot blood was frothing and bubbling in his throat. He looked up and Achilles was standing over him.

"Please," said Hector, "I beg you, do not let the Greek dogs tear my flesh by your hollow ships. Return my body to my own people."

Achilles spat at him.

"You killed Patroclus. I will not drive the dogs from your flesh, not for any ransom."

He put his foot onto Hector's face and tore out the dripping barbed spear. Hector stretched his hands toward the nourishing earth and darkness descended on his eyes.

Achilles dragged the body of Hector to his chariot. He stripped it of his armor. He threw the armor into the car of his chariot. He lifted one of Hector's feet. He pulled a knife from his belt and pierced a hole through Hector's heel, between the sinew and the bone. He did the same with the other foot. Then he threaded a length of oxhide thong through the two holes. He knotted it tightly. He tied the other end to the back of his chariot.

He leapt into the car, whipped his four horses to a gallop and drove them three times around the city walls of Troy. The body of Hector bounced behind. The face of Hector tore a furrow into the earth.

On the city walls, on the turrets and towers the people of Troy stood and stared. They were appalled, mesmerized. And it was only when Achilles drove his horses across the plain and through the gates of the wooden palisade that their tears came, and they gave themselves over to dark despair.

When Achilles and his men returned to the Greek camp they set to work. Bone-weary from battle, still dressed in their armor, they cut down trees and built a pyre a hundred feet in width and length. On top of the heap they put Patroclus. They poured on oil, wine and honey. They killed goats, horses and cattle. They surrounded the corpse with the dead.

As the flames consumed his friend, Achilles spoke.

"Brothers! Patroclus goes across the river. Soon I will join him, the gods decree. Swear to me that when I die you'll burn me too. You'll mingle my ashes with those of Patroclus so that we will be together for all time."

Achilles's tears spattered onto his bloodstained armor.

The Greeks rode their chariots around the flaming pyre. Then Achilles and his men held a feast in honor of Patroclus . . . and all through those tender celebrations, Achilles kept running into the shadows to kick the battered corpse of Hector, stamp upon his limbs, spit into his face, as the dogs gnawed at his flesh.

The corpses of two young men: Hector and Patroclus. Both had been killed in battle. Stripped of their armor they were so alike in death that one of them could have been mistaken for the other.

Inside his painted palace, old Priam, the white-bearded father of Troy, sat on his throne as still and silent as a statue. For three days he had touched neither food nor drink. His only movement was the trickling of tears down his cheeks and his beard.

Then, suddenly, he lifted his head and spoke. "Achilles cannot be altogether a godless man. And surely he loves his own father, old Peleus. I will go to him myself. I will go to the Greek camp and I will beg him, in the name of his father, to return the body of Hector. I will offer him Hector's weight in sparkling yellow gold."

Queen Hecuba buried her face in her hands.

"Listen to him! The old man has gone mad! The mighty gods have addled his wits. That wild beast, that savage animal will tear him limb from limb, just as he has destroyed our own son."

But Priam took no notice of his wife. He got to his feet and walked to the treasure room of his palace. He lifted the lids from chests and coffers and began to make a great pile of gold: arm-rings radiant, shields shining, burnished battle-vests, decorated drinking vessels. He piled gold upon gold upon gold.

Paris followed him and watched him working. Then he said,

"Father, you cannot go to the Greek camp alone. At least take me with you."

The old king shook his head.

"No. I go alone."

"Then take someone with you."

Priam turned to his son.

"Very well. If you insist, I shall take little Polyxena with me."

And so that night, as the sky brightened with stars, Priam and his youngest daughter, Princess Polyxena, who was only seventeen years old, wrapped themselves in black cloaks. They drew black hoods over their faces. Two horses had been harnessed to a cart that was filled with gold. Father and daughter climbed up onto the seat of the cart. Priam shook the reins and they clattered through the cobbled streets of the city. The Scaean gates were opened.

They made their way across the plain as a full moon slid up into the sky. They passed churned earth, splintered trees and shattered chariots. They passed dead horses, swollen with decay, their hooves pointing up to the stars. They passed the bodies of foot soldiers, some still sticky with blood and others no more than tatters of skin clinging to bleached bones. Everywhere there was the scuttling of rats and the fighting of dogs over carrion. Everything was black and gray and silver in the moonlight.

At last they reached the wooden gates of the palisade. Some god or goddess must have been watching over them. The gates were open and the sentinels were fast asleep.

They entered the Greek camp. They threaded between makeshift huts, and ships

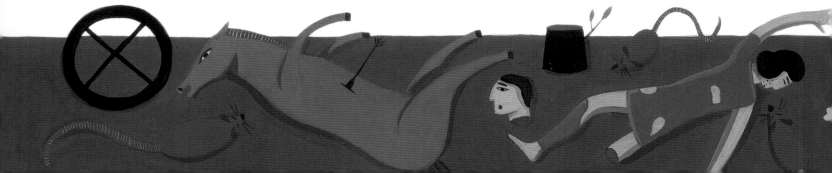

whose curved prows stretched high above their heads, dark against the silver sky. They made their way across the white sand to the sea's edge where the waves crashed and dragged. They came to the hut of Achilles.

Priam clambered down from the cart. Princess Polyxena stayed with the gold. The old king lifted the latch and pushed open the door of the hut. He saw Achilles. He was sitting alone, staring at the ground. Priam ran forward. He threw himself onto the floor at Achilles's feet. He curled his left arm over Achilles's knees. He kissed the man-slaying hands that had so recently been the death of his own son. Then Priam spoke.

"It is a father's joy to hear his son returning home. First he catches the click and creak of a door opening, and then the thud as dust or mud is stamped from sandals. Then he listens for the sound of a shield as it is thrown clattering onto the ground. And then he hears a snatch of song. And then perhaps he sees his son striding into his hall, pouring himself a cup of wine, gulping it down and wiping the froth from his lips with the back of his hand . . . Achilles, even now as I am speaking, your father, old Peleus, will be longing for your return. He will be dreaming of your return. A return that I will never see. At least give me the body of Hector. I will pay for it with his weight in sparkling yellow gold."

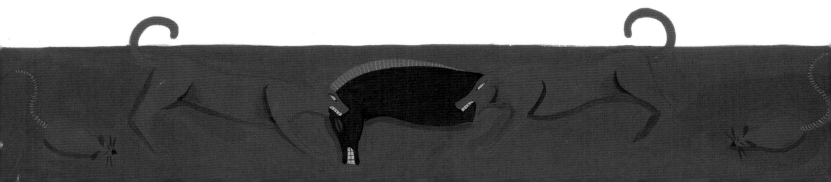

In that moment it seemed to Achilles that this was his own father. For years he'd cursed Priam as the bullish sire of a brutal brood, but before him he saw a trembling old man. An old man scarred with care. He saw white hair, white beard, trembling hands: a father who had lost a son.

Achilles's eyes filled with tears. He put his hands on the old man's shoulders and they wept together as though they were family, as though they shared the same sorrow. Achilles wept until the tears would come no longer.

"How much you've suffered!" said Achilles. "Such pain would crush my spirit. And you must have a heart of iron to walk among your mortal foes. How blessed we seemed when we were born, Hector and I. Both of us were born the sons of kings, but both of us were cursed by the gods. My father, too, will soon discover he has outlived his son. I grant your wish. You'll have his body. And for however long you need to grieve him, I'll hold back these armies. I'll wait, and watch for funeral smoke."

Achilles ordered that a weighing scales be built outside the hut, each pan the size of a grown man. Then, wrapped in a

woolen shroud, the corpse of Hector was carried across and laid
at their feet.

Priam dropped to his knees beside the body of Hector.
One by one he folded back the layers of the woolen shroud. As
he did so, golden Apollo looked down from the heavens and
took pity on the old man. With one gesture of his hand he
undid all the desecration, so that when Priam folded back the
last layer he saw Hector's face in all of its beauty, as though he
was asleep. He kissed Hector's forehead. He kissed his eyes
and his lips and his tears splashed onto Hector's face.

Then the body of Hector was lifted and laid tenderly in one
of the pans of the wooden scales. Princess Polyxena climbed
down from the cart and began to carry the gold across and set it
in the other pan. She piled gold upon gold upon gold. But
when the cart was empty, Hector's body was still heavier. The
princess unfastened the necklaces from her throat and threw
them into the pan. She pulled the golden bracelets and bangles
from her wrists and threw them into the pan. She pulled the
rings from her fingers.

Achilles watched Polyxena. He couldn't take his eyes from her. A strange, unexpected thing was happening to him. He was falling in love with her.

With the very last of her rings Hector's body lifted and slowly, perfectly, the two pans of the scales balanced. His body was carried to the cart. Achilles bowed to Priam and Polyxena.

"Old man, princess, sit down and eat with me before you go."

A table was set and the three of them sat down together. Meat, bread, wine and honey cakes were served. Achilles broke the white bread with his own hands and offered it to them. When the food was finished he reached across the table. He took Priam's hand and kissed it.

"Old man, we mortals are wretched things, and the gods who know no care have written sorrow into the pattern of our lives."

Then he took Polyxena's hand. As he kissed it he pushed a ring onto one of her fingers: a golden ring in the shape of a curling arrow whose sharp point touched its feathered tail. She looked at it in astonishment. Then she and her father got up to their feet. They climbed onto the seat of the cart. Priam shook the reins and they made their way out of the Greek camp, across the plain and back to the city of Troy.

For ten days there were funeral games in honor of Hector. On the eleventh day, a huge funeral pyre was built outside the city walls and the body of Hector was laid on top of it. All day the heat of the fire's heart consumed the house of bone. When all had been reduced to smoldering ashes, Paris gathered the charred bones of his brother. He put them into a golden casket. Stones were piled over the casket. Earth was piled over the stones. The people of Troy, their heads bowed in sorrow, walked away from the burial mound and returned to the city. Only Andromache remained. She knelt beside her husband's grave.

"Sweet Hector," she said. "I could not even hold your hand when you died."

Next day the terrible tumult resumed. At the forefront of the battle, Achilles severed heads with every stroke of his sword. But that night he wrapped himself in a black cloak and slipped out of the Greek camp. He made his way from shadow to shadow until he could see Troy. He scanned the walls of the city, desperate for a glimpse of Polyxena.

Day after day he fought. Night after night he prowled. Eventually, exasperated, he bribed a Trojan foot-soldier to carry a message to Polyxena, begging her to meet him in an ancient olive grove outside the city walls.

When the letter was pressed into her hands she opened it. She read the words. She remembered Achilles. She remembered his lithe beauty. She looked at the ring on her finger and she was filled with longing for him.

That night, under cover of darkness, she wrapped herself in her black cloak and hood. She made her way through the shadowed streets. She slipped through a secret gate in the city wall. She crossed the plain and approached the olive grove. Some of the trees were still standing, some lay splintered on the ground.

A figure stepped out of the shadows. She ran forward into his arms. And those hands that had been the death of her brother caressed her tenderly. Achilles threw his cloak onto the ground. They lay down together and talked, laughed, kissed.

But nothing is hidden from the eyes of the mighty immortals. Aphrodite called to golden Apollo.

"Apollo, come and look at this! Look what I have brought about."

Apollo looked down and shook his head.

"Shameless Polyxena. Shameless, shameless Aphrodite."

"But Apollo, don't you understand?" said Aphrodite. "This is our chance! Go and tell Paris that his sister has taken a lover, a Greek lover. Tell him to follow her tomorrow night with a bow and a quiverful of arrows. I'll put what words I can into Polyxena's mouth."

Suddenly Apollo understood. He threw back his head and shouted with laughter. Swift as thought he flew into the city. He entered the palace of Prince Paris. He entered the bedchamber where Paris was lying asleep in Helen's arms. He entered Paris's dreams. He whispered.

"Paris, did you know that your sister Polyxena has taken a lover? A Greek lover! Follow her tomorrow night with a bow and a quiverful of arrows."

Paris woke up with the words echoing in his mind. All the next day, he watched Polyxena, but she gave no hint, no clue, no indication. Then, at nightfall, he saw her wrapping the black cloak about herself. He seized a bow and some arrows. He followed her through the streets, through the secret gate, across the plain. He saw the olive grove. He saw a figure step out of the shadows. He saw his sister run into his arms.

Then, Paris felt a cold shudder from the nape of his neck to the root of his spine. Achilles! It was Achilles! He flattened himself against the ground. He buried his face in the dust, hardly daring to breathe. As he lay there he could hear the lovers talking and laughing. He heard them lying down together. Very slowly he lifted his head. He peered over the trunk of a fallen tree. He could see the lovers clearly in the moonlight. He could see Achilles's shoulders, the small of his back, the backs of his legs and his heels. Then he heard his sister speak.

"My love, I don't understand. This war has lasted for nearly as long as I can remember. It has lasted since I was seven years old. And you have always been in the thick of it. And yet you are unscratched. There are no marks on your body. No scars, no scratches, no bruises . . . "

Achilles laughed.

"Polyxena, when I was a baby my mother carried me to the dark waters of the River Styx. She dipped me into the river. Wherever the water touched me I am invulnerable. The only place I can be harmed is where she held me: my heels."

Paris fitted an arrow to his bow. He drew the bowstring back. He loosed the arrow. It whistled through the air.

And it would have gone wide of its mark if golden Apollo had not been watching and waiting. The archer god seized the arrow in his hand. He ran forward, invisible, and plunged the point of it into Achilles's heel.

A great shudder went through Achilles's body. The life went out of him in one breath.

Paris leapt to his feet.

"Achilles is dead!"

He ran back to the city. He ran from street to street.

"Achilles is dead! Achilles is dead!"

In every house lanterns were lit. People came pouring into the streets.

"Achilles is dead! Achilles is dead!"

In the Greek camp, Odysseus was woken by a great commotion. Fearful of a Trojan ambush, he searched for the source of the sound and found himself outside Achilles's stables. He opened the doors.

The white horses were kicking the air with their front legs, rolling their eyes. Odysseus harnessed them to a chariot. They took him across the blasted battlefield to an olive grove near the walls of the city.

He saw a woman. She seemed to be Trojan by the way she wore her hair. She was kneeling, sobbing, and before her in the grass was the corpse of Achilles! Achilles was dead!

He gathered up the body, clambered into the chariot and back to the camp.

"Achilles is dead! Achilles is dead!"

The Trojans followed Paris out of the city. They followed him across the plain to the olive grove. But there was no sign of Achilles. There was only Princess Polyxena. A seventeen-year-old girl, shaking with sobs, staring at the golden ring on her finger as it dribbled blood down the back of her hand. The blood was trickling down her arm. It was dripping from her elbow onto the nourishing earth.

When Odysseus returned to the camp everyone was awake. They followed him with flaming torches from the gates to the gathering place. He lifted the body of Achilles and laid it on the ground. The men gasped. It was beautiful. All through his life Achilles's face had been twisted with emotion. Now he was past all the cares that had tortured him. As they feasted on his beauty, his mother came, her face shrouded in a veil. She gathered up the lifeless body of her son and sobbed. It was an awful thing to see the extremity of her grief. The men left her alone. She built a pyre. As the flames

consumed the body of Achilles, she remembered the happiest day of her life – her wedding day. How full of hope she'd been! She remembered all the fateful wedding gifts: the spear, the breastplate, the golden ring, the four white horses, the ant army . . . and then she remembered the last gift.

She went to Achilles's hut. There it was, squatting in the corner, gathering shadows, the gift of the last of all gods, Hades. The black urn with the silver image of the three Fates inlaid into its front.

The first, who spins out the thread of a life.

The second, who measures out its length.

And the third, who cuts the thread and ends the life.

She put the ashes of Patroclus into the urn. She went out to the pyre and mingled the ashes of her son with those of his friend. She carried the precious urn out of the camp, to a headland that overlooks the sea. She buried the urn there. She heaped rocks over the grave. When she'd finished she said,

"My dear son. Not for you the stretching shadows. Not for you the ripening grape. Not for you the joy of children. You chose glory."

·THE·WOODEN·HORSE·

·91·

Next day, there was no sign of mother or child. Odysseus called a meeting in the gathering place.

"Achilles is dead. If he could not breach these walls, then force of arms never will. I have a plan. Years ago, when we Greeks first heard of Helen's beauty, we gathered in the palace of her foster father, hoping to win her hand in marriage. He made us swear an oath of loyalty over the severed limbs of a stallion. This business will end as it began – with a horse."

Odysseus's men set to work. They cut down trees. They split and sawed the wood. They carved legs, flanks, belly, neck, back, mane and head. They set it on a huge platform. Odysseus and twelve of his bravest warriors climbed inside the hollow belly. A secret trapdoor was closed behind them. The enormous wooden horse was painted black from head to hoof and golden words were emblazoned on its flank.

Then, after nightfall, the Greek army burned its camp. Every hut, shop, storehouse and temple was reduced to smoldering ash. They dragged their ships down to the water and sailed along the coast, far out of sight of the city of Troy.

The next morning, as the dawn took her golden throne, the people of Troy looked across the plain and saw that the Greeks were gone.

"Look! Now that they've lost Achilles they've given up and gone home. The siege is over at last!"

They rubbed their eyes and looked again. In the middle of the drifting smoke of the deserted camp there was something strange, towering dark against the shimmering waves of the sea.

The Scaean gates were thrown open and the Trojans – men, women and children – hurried across the plain. Soon they were on the seashore and the great horse was towering over their heads. They walked around it, staring at it, amazed. There were words written along its flank.

A GIFT TO THE GODDESS ATHENE

The priests and seers laughed.

"The cowards have fled and they fear the anger of the goddess of war and wisdom. They've left this horse as an offering to her."

"We will carry it into the city," said King Priam, "and set it outside her temple."

The people of Troy lifted the huge platform onto their shoulders. They carried the horse across the plain and through the streets to the temple of Athene.

And then the victory feast began. Trestle tables were laden with food and drink. Every man, woman and child ate and drank until their bellies were hanging over their belts and their heads were swimming with red wine. As the moon climbed into the sky they staggered to their beds and fell into the sweet, oblivious balm of sleep.

When even the dogs were sleeping, the belly of the horse swung open and down tumbled a rope ladder. Odysseus and his men crept through the silent streets and opened the Scaean gates from the inside.

The Greek army, under cover of darkness, had returned. Soon they were pouring into the city, swords and spears poised, ready to spill Trojan blood.

The immortal gods and goddesses looked down from the high slopes of Mount Olympus.

Golden Apollo watched his city burn like a blazing torch, with red flames and yellow flames rising up into the sky like flickering snakes – and he remembered the founding of his beautiful city.

Zeus, the Cloud Compeller, watched the Greeks as they flung Astyanax, Hector's baby son, from the high city walls – and he remembered the beautiful child, weeping and laughing in his father's arms.

Aphrodite looked down and saw the bleeding body of Prince Paris, with red-haired Menelaus's spear in his heart – and she remembered the beautiful young man who had chosen her on the slopes of Mount Ida.

Hera looked down and saw the turrets and towers of Troy crashing into the streets; Athene looked down and saw that Helen had been restored to her rightful husband – and both of them remembered the moment when Paris had chosen Aphrodite over them.

Then Eris, goddess of strife, spoke.

"Just think, all of this because of one golden apple!"

And Aphrodite took the apple out of her pocket, looked at it and said nothing.

And even today, when all that remains of the city of Troy is broken stone on a windy hill at the foot of Mount Ida, there is a tree growing beside a heap of rocks on a headland that overlooks the blue sea. There is a tree growing from the grave of Achilles. Maybe you'll see it yourself one day.

The branches that stretch toward the ocean, toward distant Greece, are green and shimmering with leaves. The branches that stretch toward the ruined city have withered and died before their time.

Barefoot Books
step inside a story

Hugh Lupton

has been a central figure in the British storytelling revival for more than thirty years. He tells myths, legends and folk tales from many cultures. His many books include *Tales of Wisdom and Wonder*, *The Story Tree*, *Tales of Mystery and Magic* and his novel *The Ballad of John Clare*. He lives with his wife, Liz, in Norfolk, England.

Daniel Morden

has been a professional storyteller since 1989. His book *Dark Tales from the Woods* won the Tír na nÓg Children's Book Prize in 2007. In 2006, Daniel and Hugh received the Classical Association's Award for "the most significant contribution to the public understanding of the classics." Daniel lives with his family in Abergavenny, Wales.

Carole Hénaff

is always inspired by her travels and is never without her sketchbook. She studied theatrical literature in Paris before moving to Barcelona to study graphic design and illustration. Carole has illustrated children's books in France and Spain, including *Smara*, which was awarded the Isaac Díaz Pardo Prize for Best Illustrated Book, 2006. She has also illustrated *The Arabian Nights* for Barefoot Books.